João Lino

Playing at creating

1ª edition

2023

Copy editor

Júlia Bastos

Images

Claudia Campoy

Cover design

Claudia Campoy

Graphic design and layout

João Lino

International Cataloging Data in Publication

(Câmara Brasileira do Livro, SP, Brasil)

Playing at creating/João Lino – 2023

Bibliography

ISBN - 978-65-00-70345-0

1. Family 2. Education 3. Creativity

Dedication

I dedicate this book to my mother who taught me how to build my first toy when I was 6 years old, to my father who taught me how to do things the right way - as he used to say: "Doing it wrong is three jobs, to do it, to undo iit and to do it again" - and to my sisters, who have always supported me in everything I've done in life.

Sumário

Presentation

According to the 2020 World Economic Forum report, the future job market will require cognitive skills such as problem-solving, creativity, critical thinking, leadership, and teamwork. To develop these skills in children as young as four years old, the book 'Playing to Create' has been launched. It presents a simple and economical four-week experience for parents to assemble toys with their children.

The book suggests four easy-to-assemble toys: Tweezers, a Ball Launcher, a Fishing Game, and an Equilibrist Butterfly. Each of them can be completed in a few minutes by an adult. By assembling these toys, parents encourage their children's creativity and imagination, allowing them to discover new ways of thinking and communicating.

The book also provides an opportunity for parents and children to learn together and have fun in a collaborative, creative, and safe environment. We believe that this experience will help prepare children for the future while strengthening the bond between parents and children.

Why invest in children's creativity?

Stimulating creativity and other natural abilities in children is crucial to prepare them for future challenges that will arise due to new technologies, such as Artificial Intelligence. As we approach an increasingly technological world, it is essential that children develop solid cognitive skills from an early age.

These abilities, such as logical reasoning, problem-solving and creativity, are essential for them to adapt and thrive in a constantly changing environment.

By strengthening these skills, children learn to analyze information, make decisions and find innovative solutions. In addition, cognitive skills also help to think critically and understand the ethical and social implications of technology.

By promoting cognitive development from an early age, parents and educators empower children to deal with the rapid transformations that technology brings. This involves offering diverse experiences, encouraging curiosity, stimulating problem-solving and cultivating imagination.

By investing in the cognitive development of children, we are empowering them to become creative, adaptable individuals prepared to face challenges and take advantage of the opportunities that new technologies offer.

We need to prepare for a future in which children can make the most of technological innovations while maintaining their ability to think critically and contribute to society.

Introduction

for parents and children

Activities to develop children's creativity. Suitable for parents with children aged 4 to 6 years old.

20 years ago I started making toys at home for two reasons: for my son and to relax my mind. Since then, this activity has become a passion.

In my childhood toys were much simpler. I remember playing with friends with a wooden cart. We would tie a string and pull it so the car would go behind us.

Back then my mother worked as a seamstress to help with the household expenses, so there was always a pile of empty thread spools for us to play with. She taught me how to make a "tractor" out of one of these spools, and the assembly was simple.

Toy - tractor with a spool. If the QR Code doesn't work, it could be because the author removed the video from YouTube.

I would cut a piece of candle, make a hole in the center by turning the tip of a knife to remove the paraffin, thread a rubber band through the hole in the candle and the spool, and secure the ends with matchsticks. Then, I would spin the matchstick to wind the rubber band, place the toy on the floor, and it would start walking very slowly. If there was any obstacle, the toy would go over it, as long as it wasn't too high.

What I liked most about that toy was when the spool slipped for some reason and the matchstick went to the opposite side of the movement. It was interesting to see the stick move very slowly into position and the toy to move again.

After learning how to make this toy, pulling the wooden cart with a string lost its fun, as my car could drive on its own.

Attention!

The world is undergoing radical changes.

Have you heard about *ChatGPT*? If you haven't heard it, read the answer he gave me when I asked: "what is chatgpt?"

I am *ChatGPT*, a large and advanced language model powered by OpenAI. I was trained with large amounts of textual data to generate relevant and coherent answers to a wide variety of questions and topics.

My goal is to help answer your questions, provide information, and help with tasks that can be accomplished using natural language. I am available 24 hours a day, 7 days a week and can help you in many areas, such as education, science, technology, among others.

Briefly, *ChatGPT* is a language model (GPT - Generative Pre-trained Transformer) that uses Artificial Intelligence with the ability to generate texts, answer questions, translate languages and much more, making it a useful tool for students, researchers and professionals in different areas!

If you still don't know ChatGPT, go to the link https://chat.openai.com/chat, just enter an email address and choose a password. Important to remember: access is free for personal use!

Technologies such as Artificial Intelligence, Robotics, Big Data, Machine Learning, 3D Printer, Augmented Reality, Virtual Reality, Cloud Computing, Quantum Computing, Electric Vehicles, Autonomous Vehicles, IoT - Internet of Things, Drones, Blockchain, 5G, e-commerce, Nanotechnologies, Biotechnology and Renewable Energy are transforming the world faster and faster.

In the coming years, many professions are likely to disappear, reduce supply or change their nature, for example, supermarket cashier, driver, telemarketing attendant, laboratory technician, accountant, architect, lawyer, journalist, teacher, etc.

The World Economic Forum (WEF) regularly publishes reports on the future of jobs around the world. In 2020, the WEF published "The Future of Jobs Report 2020", which analyzed the trends of 15 sectors in 26 economies in the world.

The report predicts that automation and artificial intelligence will have a significant impact on the job market, with 85 million jobs being directly affected by 2025, but also predicts the creation of 97 million new jobs in emerging sectors. However, the report points out that new jobs will require different skills than are currently needed, and that there may be a large gap between the skills people have today and those that will be needed in the near future.

In summary, the WEF report highlights the importance of developing these skills to ensure future employability.

The report also identifies what key skills will be needed, including cognitive skills, such as problem solving, creativity, critical thinking, and socio emotional skills such as emotional intelligence, leadership and teamwork.

While artificial intelligence and other technologies could profoundly change the job market, creativity will remain a valuable skill. Here are some ways creativity can help children's futures:

Adaptability: it can help children cope better in an ever-changing environment. With the ability to think outside the box, they can find creative solutions to problems and challenges that come their way.

Innovation: children who are encouraged to think creatively can acquire the ability to develop innovative solutions to local and global problems.

Communication: through artistic and creative practice, children can develop visual and verbal communication skills that will be valuable in any career.

Emotional well-being: creativity can have a positive impact on emotional well-being. More confident people tend to have healthier and more satisfying lives.

How to encourage children's creativity?

Playing at creating!

This book aims to present an experience for parents with children between 4 and 6 years old. Four manual activities will be suggested to help in the development of children's creativity. It is a simple, cost-effective, four-week experience that allows parents to experience the fun and educational art of building toys with their children.

From the earliest years of a child, the parents are the ones who transmit values, habits and knowledge that will be remembered throughout life. They also create the environment in which the child will develop and learn, through affection, patience, dedication and example.

Parents are the first ones to have contact with their children's abilities, difficulties and interests, making them the most capable ones to offer personalized education adapted to their needs. They are also responsible for creating the environment of trust and security necessary for the child to feel free to learn by trying new things.

It is important that the child observes one of the parents putting the toys together, as this will stimulate their curiosity and creativity. We suggest that parents build one toy a week, allowing the child time to play and exercise their imagination, while learning to deal with the anxiety of waiting for the next toy.

Parental involvement is essential for the development of children's creativity.

Parents who practice creative activities inspire their children to do the same!

By showing the child that it is possible to create something with limited resources, you will be encouraging them to express themselves creatively, giving them the opportunity to explore their imagination and discover new ways of thinking and communicating.

Finally, parents are the main teachers because they offer personalized instruction and create the ideal environment to encourage the pleasure of learning. By providing a creative and inspiring home environment, parents help their children develop skills that will be valuable throughout their lives.

Suggested activities

The book features four simple and fun activities: Tweezers, Ball Launcher, Fishing Game and Equilibrist Butterfly. Each one is easy to assemble, and an adult takes an average of 30 seconds to 3 minutes to complete the toy.

Next, you'll see the presentation and a detailed step-by-step to do the activities, including the list of necessary materials. But for the ideas in this book to be successful, it is recommended that parents assemble the toys together with their children, allowing them to observe and help during this process.

Do not hand over the materials for the child to do the activities!

It is important to emphasize that the suggested materials are ecological or can be recycled. Unfortunately, activities involving elastic potential energy, for example, require the use of rubber objects.

In order to facilitate the work for parents, there is a kit with pre-prepared materials to carry out these activities.

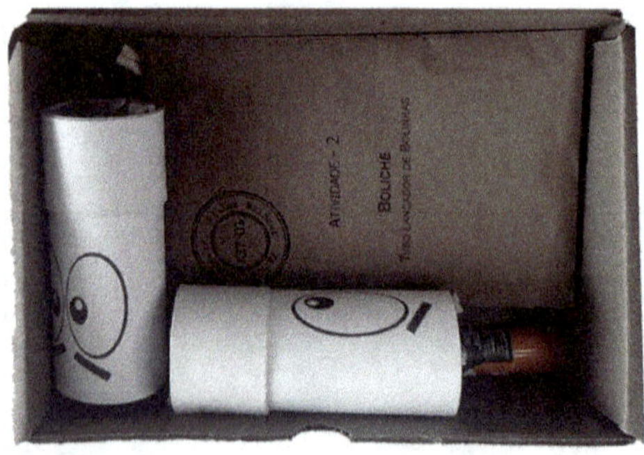

Kit for parents and children

Activity 1

Tweezers

Handling tweezers is an activity that can help in children's development, especially in motor coordination. Here are some examples of how this activity can be beneficial:

Fine motor skills: using tweezers involves precise movements, using the muscles in the hands and fingers, helping to develop dexterity and fine motor skills.

Muscle strengthening: regular use of tweezers is good for strengthening the muscles in the hands and fingers. This practice can help the child to find easier to hold and handle other objects.

Visual perception: to handle tweezers, the child needs to observe carefully to choose and pick up the object correctly, thus developing spatial perception and visual discrimination.

Sensory stimulation: the act of handling objects with tweezers can provide a pleasant sensation for the child's hands and fingers, helping to develop sensory awareness and the ability to concentrate on manual tasks.

Writing preparation: this is a useful activity to prepare children for writing, as it helps to develop the coordination and control needed to correctly hold and use a pen or pencil.

In short, using this toy is a fun and educational activity that can help a child develop fine motor skills, visual perception, and writing skills.

Material to make Tweezers

Materials that are part of the Kit "For Parents and Children"

Inside the envelope you will find **2** drawings to color, cut and paste on the clothespin; **2** colorful drawings to paste on the clothespin; **4** ice cream sticks; **2** clothespins; **2** bottle caps and **6** double-sided stickers.

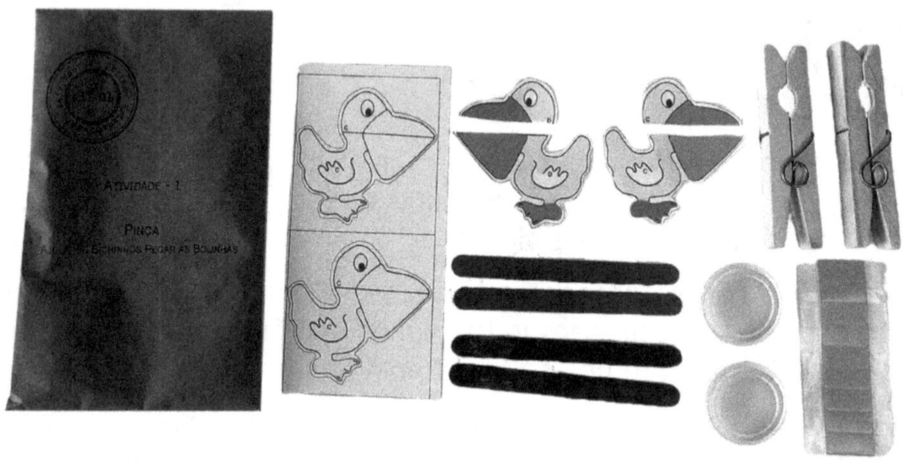

If you purchase the Kit, do not give the envelope to your children. For this experience to present positive results, the parents must assemble the toy and the child must watch and help in the assembly.

To assemble a toy, you will need the following materials:

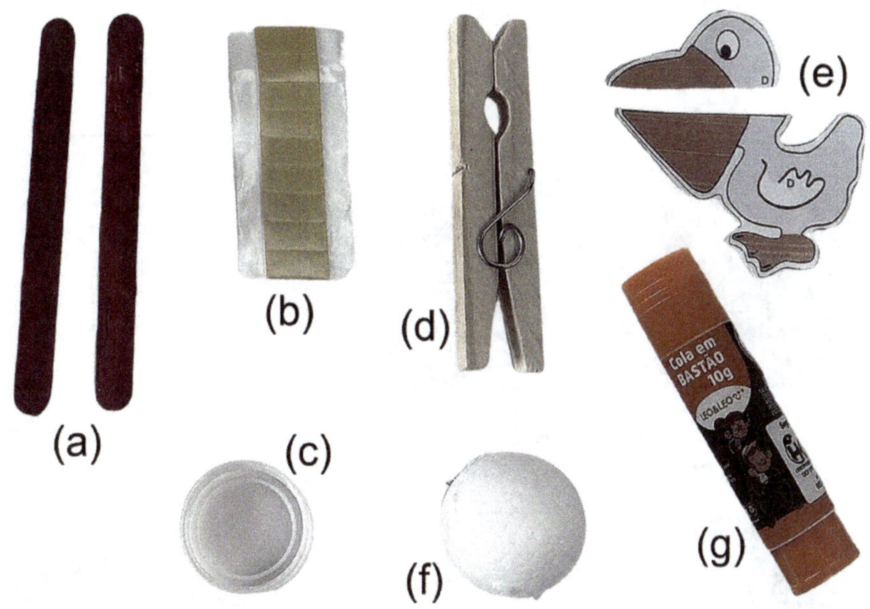

a) 2 sticks of ice cream

b) 3 double-sided stickers

c) 1 bottle cap

d) 1 clothespin

e) 1 drawing to paste on the fastener

f) 1 Styrofoam ball (in the Kit, inside the paper tubes, there are 2 Styrofoam balls)

g) glue stick

Tweezers

Step by Step

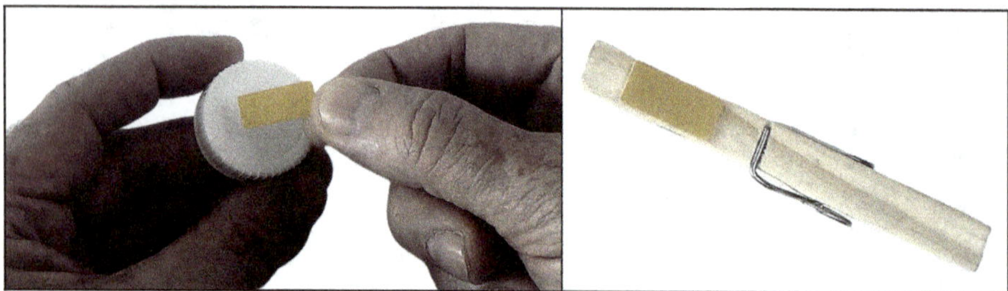

Glue 1 double-sided sticker on the bottle cap and 2 stickers on the front of the clothespin at both ends.

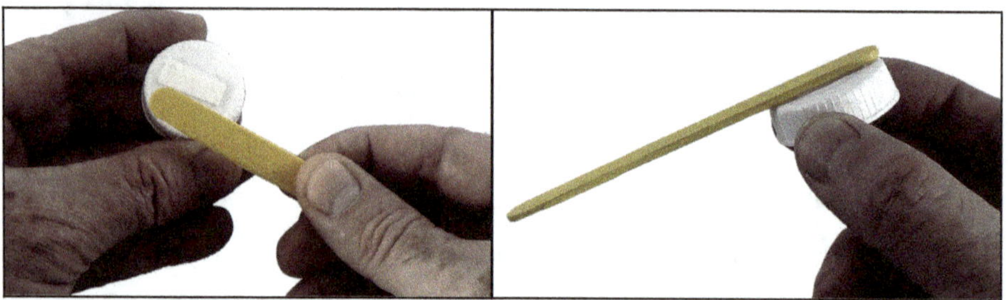

Remove the backing from the sticker on the bottle cap and stick an ice cream stick. Align the tip of this toothpick with the edge of the lid.

YouTube - step-by-step instructional video.

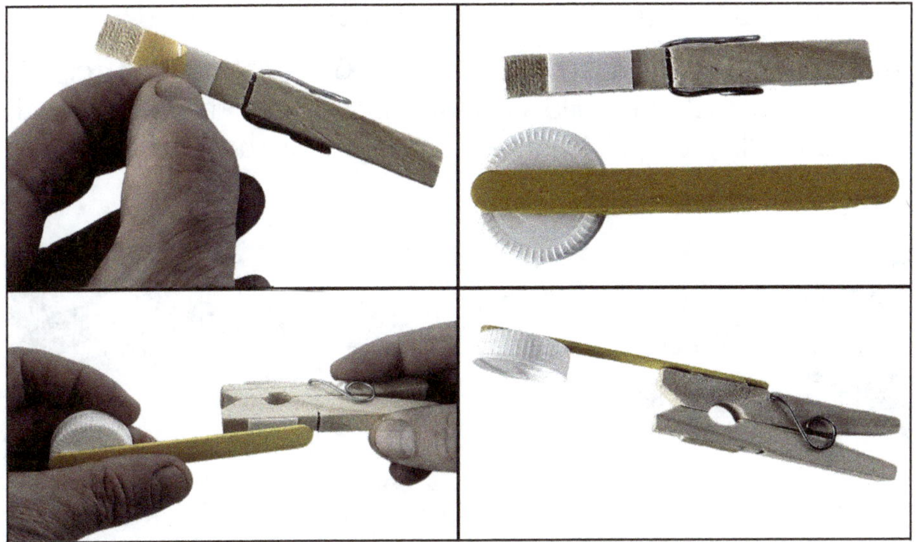

Remove the protection from one of the stickers on the clothespin and stick this ice cream stick as follows:

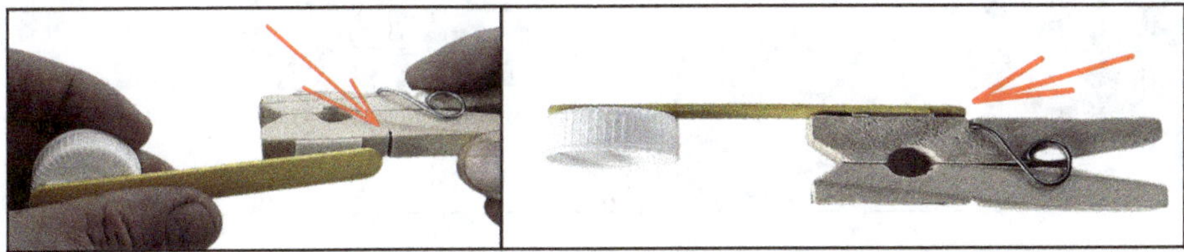

a) The bottle cap needs to face the underside of the clamp.

b) The tip of the toothpick needs to line up with the spring metal of the fastener.

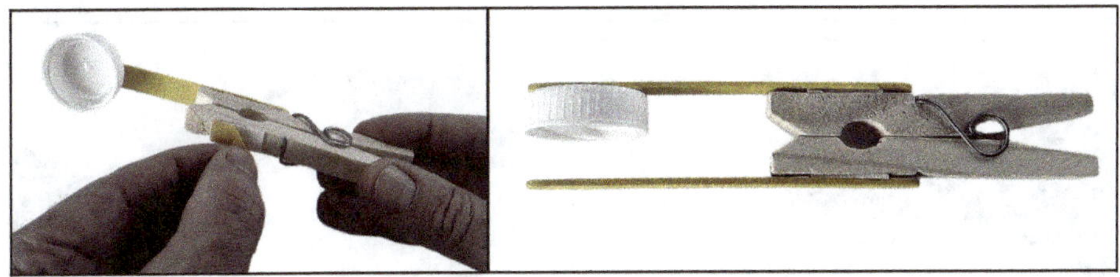

Turn the clip over, remove the adhesive backing, and stick the second ice cream stick. Align the end of this toothpick with the spring metal of the fastener.

Will the child hold the "Pinch" with the right or left hand?

Note that the drawings have a letter "**D**" (right-handed) or "**C**" (left-handed). If the child is right-handed, use the design with the letter "D", or you can paste designs on both sides of the clothespin.

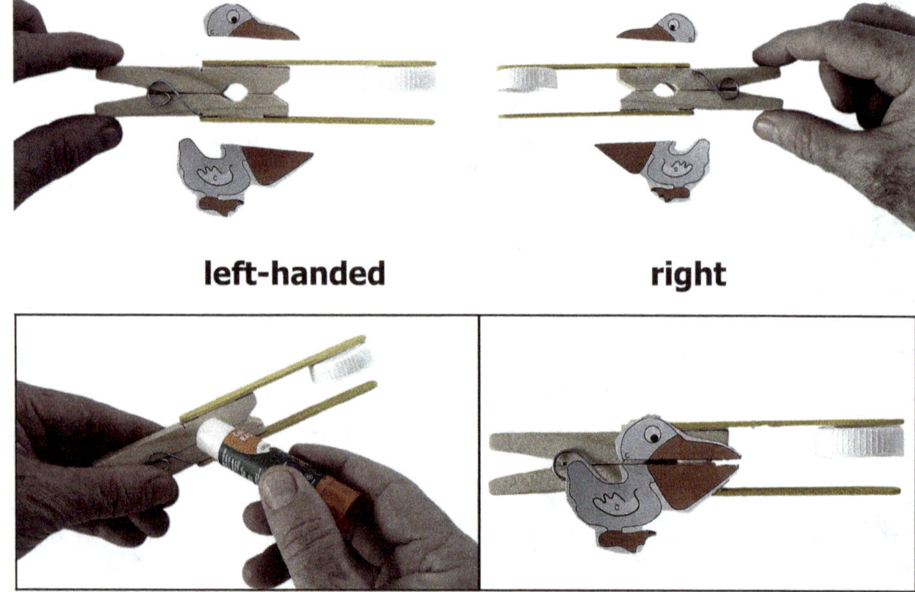

left-handed   **right**

Choose a design. Apply glue to the side of the fastener and glue the "head" to the top and the "body" to the bottom.

Teach the child to pick up objects with tweezers. For an adult it's a simple movement, for a 4 year old it's not!

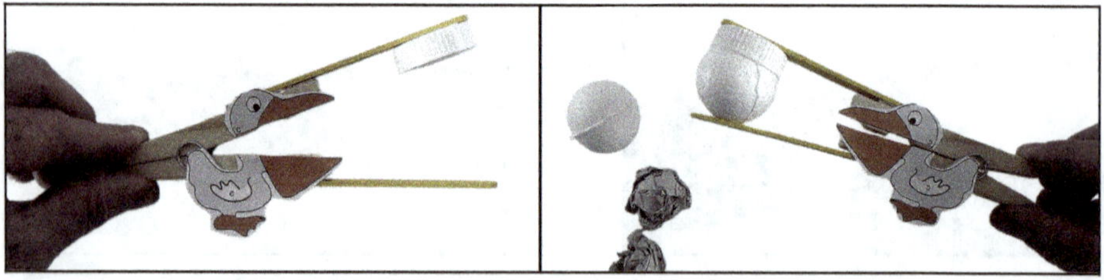

Show that when she presses the ends on the back of the fastener the front ends open and when she stops pressing the front ends close. It is important to explain these details!

Playing with a Tweezer

Transfer forceps

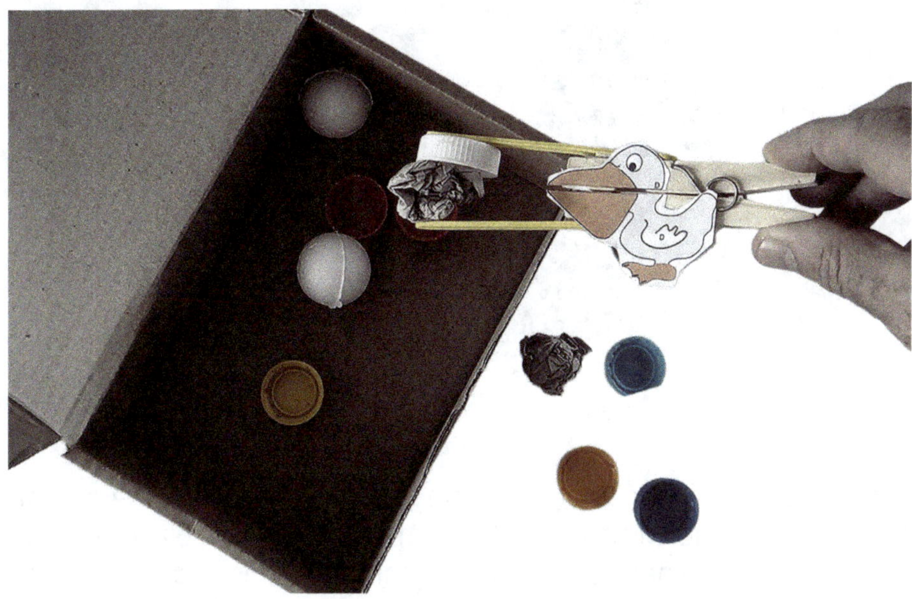

This is a very easy game, you just need to empty the kit's cardboard box so that the child can transport the balls from the outside of the box to the inside and vice versa.

Alternative polka dots

Instead of styrofoam balls, teach the child to knead the sponge paper, the one that came on top of the box, to make paper balls.

Fishing with tweezers

Fill a pot with water and place the Styrofoam balls inside it. The child can use the tweezers to "fish" the objects and place them in a separate container. Explain to the child that this is a way to pick up the balls without getting your fingers wet.

Color classification

Use bottle caps with different colors. The child can use the "tweezers" to separate the objects by color and place them in separate containers.

Activity 2

Polka Dot Launcher

A toy that launches balls can be a great tool to help a child's development in several ways:

Motor coordination: the act of putting the ball in the tube and pulling the rubber back, with more or less force adjusting the power of the throw, helps to develop hand-eye coordination and the ability to use arm and hand muscles to execute a precise movement.

Visual perception: the child needs to imagine and follow the trajectory of the ball during games, which helps to develop visual perception and the ability to anticipate movements.

Cause and effect: the child learns that pulling the balloon back and letting go launches the ball forward, which helps develop an understanding of cause and effect as well as the ability to predict outcomes.

Concentration: the child needs to focus on hitting the target, throwing or catching the balls, which helps to develop the ability to concentrate and pay attention.

Social skill: toys that can be used in a group help develop social skills, such as sharing, cooperating and following the rules of a game.

In short, this toy can help your child develop cognitive skills while having fun.

Material to make the Polka Dot Launcher

Materials that are part of the Kit "For Parents and Children"

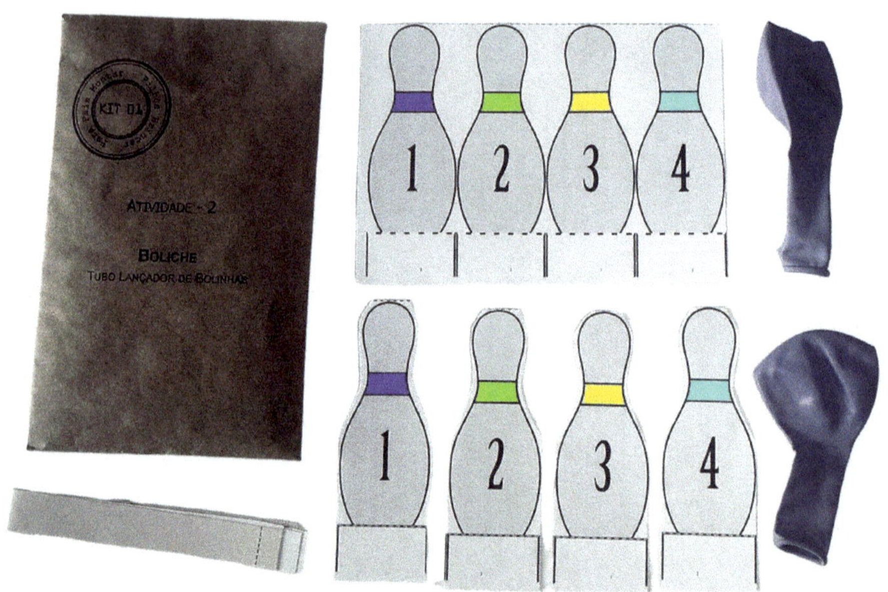

Inside the envelope you will find **1** bowling 4 pin design; **4** drawings of cut out bowling pins; **2** balloons with cut bottom and **2** adhesive strips. The balls are inside the paper tubes, they are 2 Styrofoam balls with 3.5 cm in diameter.

If you purchase the Kit, do not give the envelope to your children. For this experience to present positive results, the parents must assemble the toy and the child must watch and help in the assembly.

To assemble a toy, you will need the following materials:

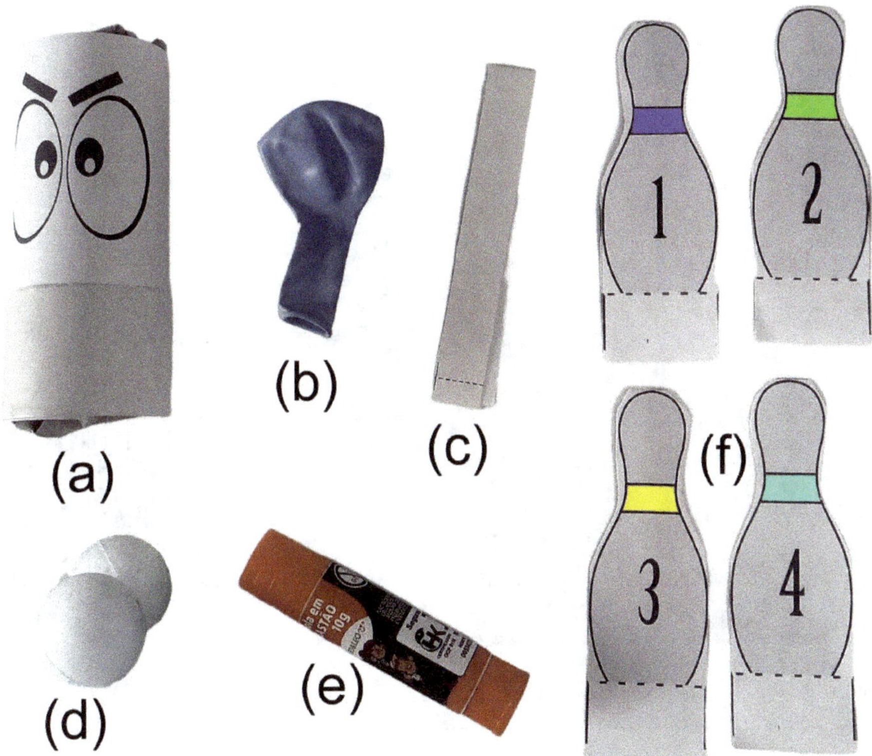

(a)

(b)

(c)

(d)

(e)

(f)

a) 1 tube

b) 1 balloon

c) 1 sticky tape

d) 1 styrofoam ball

e) glue stick

f) 4 bowling pins

Polka Dot Launcher

Step by Step

YouTube
Step-by-step
instructional video

Tie a knot in the balloon pipe.

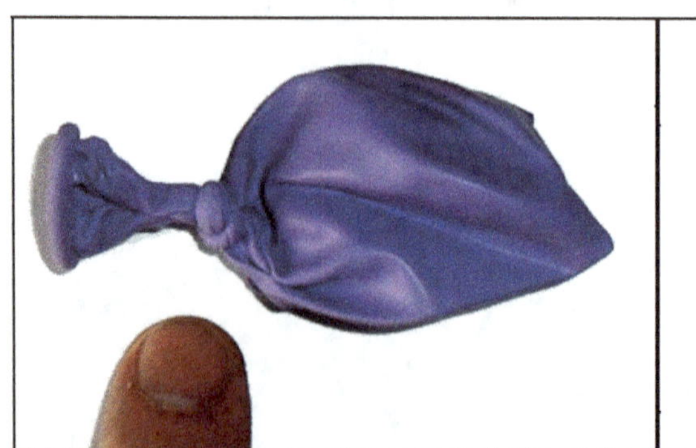

knot near body – **right**

knot near mouth - **wrong**

The knot needs to be close to the body and not close to the mouth of the balloon.

Place the tube on a flat surface in an upright position. The thickest "ring" needs to be on the top side.

Use your fingertips to open the bottom of the balloon and fit the tube. Leave the knot near the center of the tube.

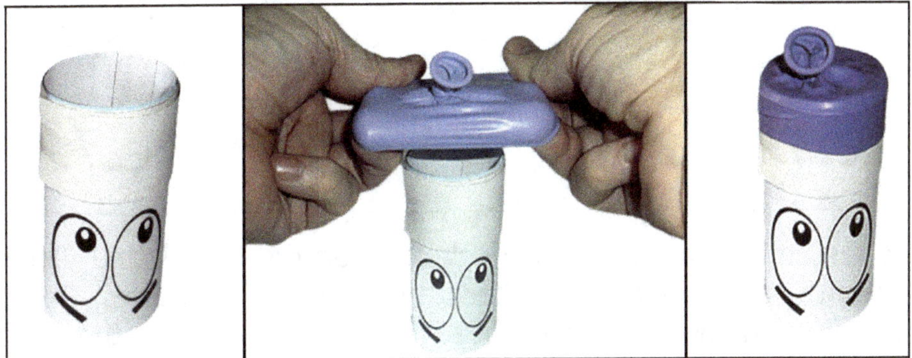

Fit the rubber around the tube.

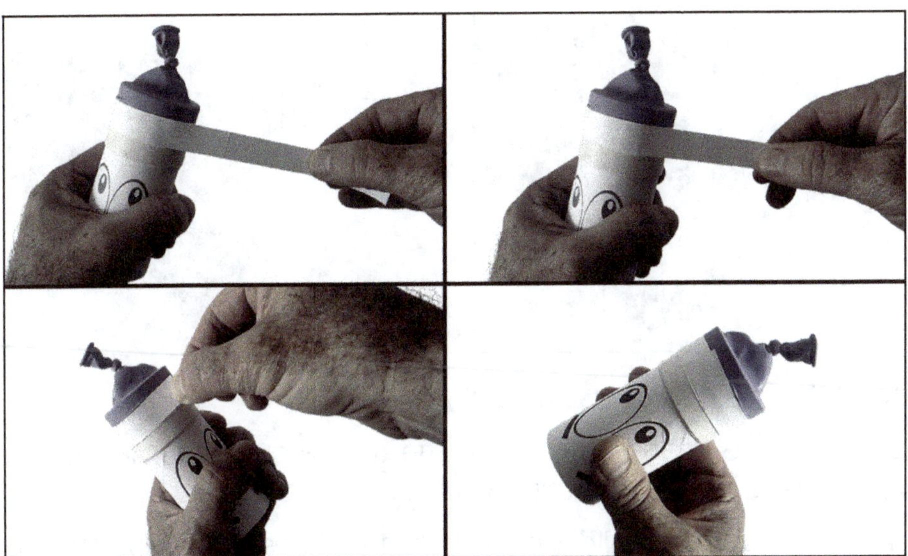

Use masking tape to secure the rubber around the tube.

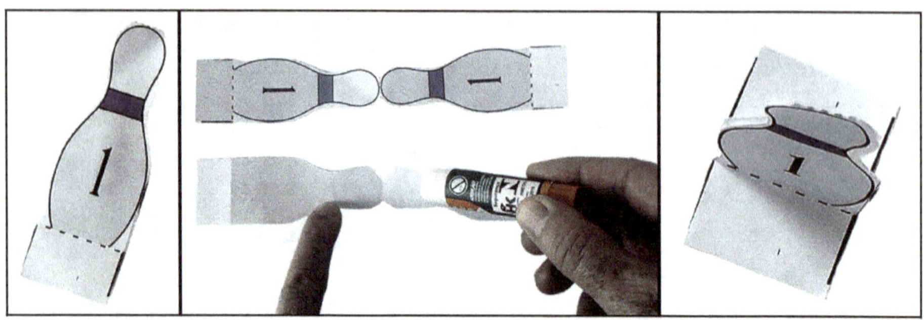

To assemble the pegs, fold the paper on the dotted lines upwards, apply glue on the back and join the two halves. Don't put glue on the ends, they need to be open to keep the pins upright.

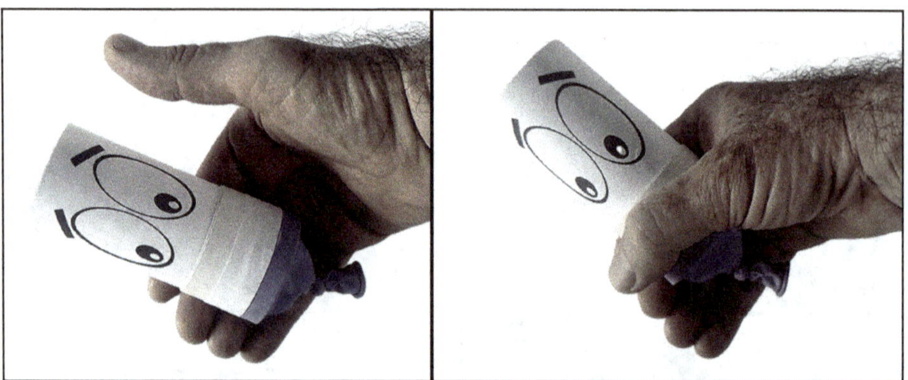

Teach the child to throw the ball.

a) If you are right-handed, hold the tube around your left hand, if you are left-handed around your right hand.

b) Explain to the child that you cannot press the tube, if you squeeze the tube it will crumple.

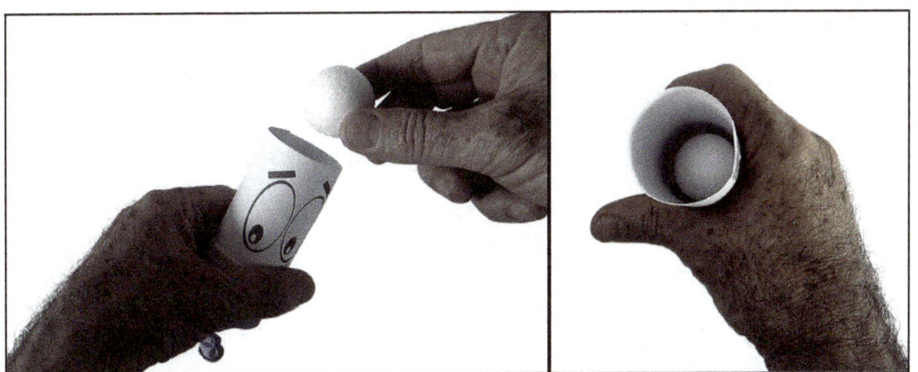

Place the ball inside the tube.

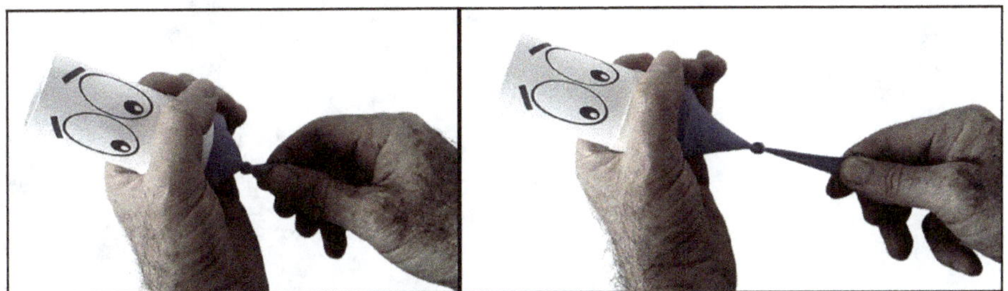

Pull the end of the balloon back, point it up and release.

Important 1

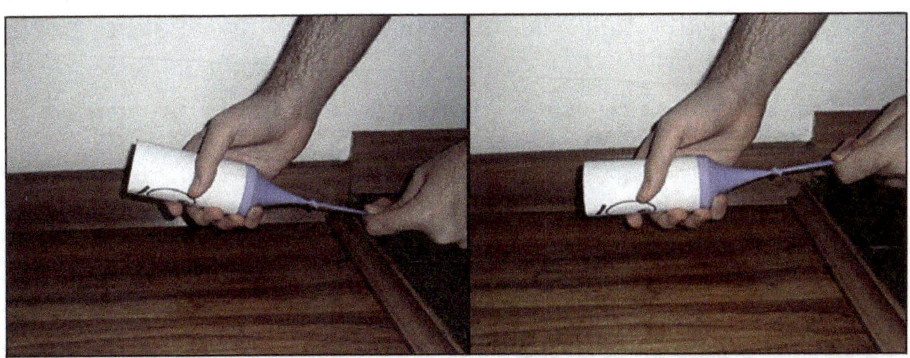

right – "mouth" up   **wrong – "mouth" down**

Guide the child on the correct way to hold the tube, the "mouth" needs to be slightly upwards, otherwise the ball will fall before being released.

Important 2

Before playing games, let the child practice throwing the ball in the air. After a few throws, show how to throw the ball forward, that is, holding the tube slightly diagonally.

Important 3

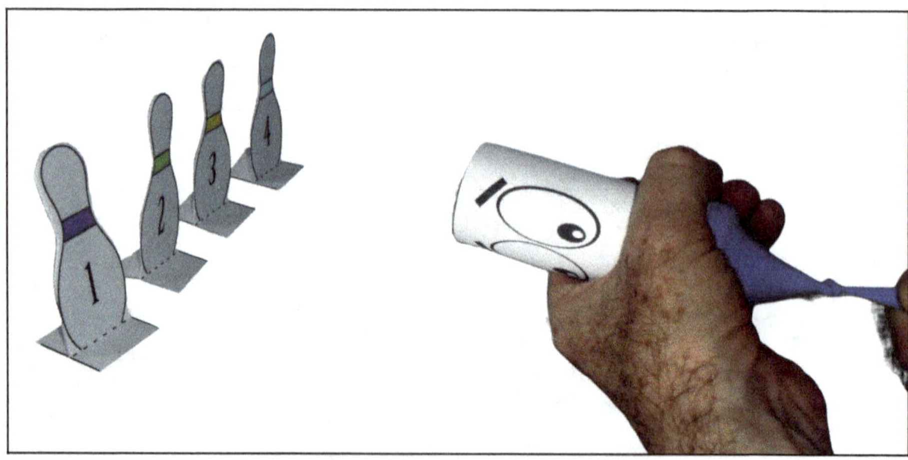

To play bowling, place the pins 2 meters away from the player and the players need to sit on the floor. If the players stand, the 'mouth' of the tube must point down towards the bowling pins. Consequently, the ball will fall out of the tube before being released.

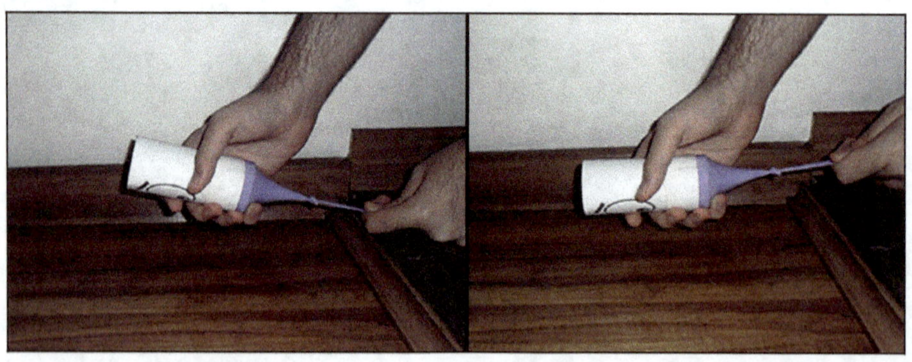

right – "mouth" up   **wrong – "mouth" down**

Games with the Polka Dot Launcher

Bowling

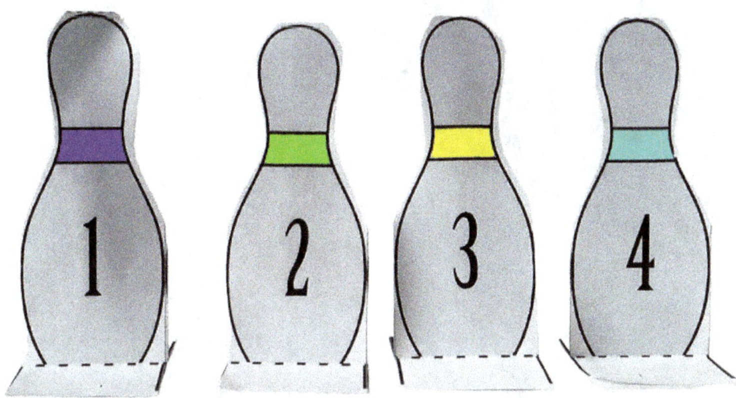

In bowling, each player uses the balls to knock down the four pins. Whoever manages to knock down more pins with fewer balls wins the game. To play, you need to sit on the floor and hold the tube slightly tilted upwards, but at the same height as the pegs.

Hit target 1

In this game, the objective is to hit the balls inside a box. It is possible to use the Kit's cardboard box, we suggest placing a cloth in the box to prevent the ball from bouncing when it falls.

Hit target 2

This game is for two players who are positioned facing each other with a distance of one or two meters. The first player places their tube in a vertical position, and the second player tries to knock down the opponent's tube by throwing the balls. Whoever knocks down the opponent's tube the most times wins the game.

Just like the game of "bowling", suggested earlier, **the players need to stay seated on the floor**.

Knock down the tower

Pass to friend

This game is for two players, the child throws the ball in the air towards the parents or a friend. The challenge is to catch the ball, preventing it from falling to the ground.

If you have paper cups available, you can use them to create a tower as a target, then knock it down with the marbles.

Caution

It is important to supervise children during play to ensure that they are in an appropriate and safe environment for this activity. For example, if the game involves throwing the ball into the air, it is possible that the child will run towards the ball without looking at what is in front of them.

Activity 3

Fishing Game

This game can be a great way to develop a 4-year-old's skills in many areas, including hand-eye coordination, memory, concentration, social skills, critical thinking, and knowledge about shapes and colors.

Motor coordination: the act of using the "fishing rod" to "fish" the magnetic squares helps develop hand-eye coordination and the ability to use arm and hand muscles to execute precise movements.

Learning shapes and colors: the game includes different images that help the child to recognize and associate colors and animals.

Critical thinking: the game with cards and pieces makes it possible to analyze the chances of losing or winning, which helps to develop problem-solving skills.

Memory: this activity was designed to challenge and exercise memory. Each time the child plays, they will try to remember details that allow them to locate different pieces individually or in pairs. For example, the child can memorize that the piece with the bent edge is the "yellow rabbit" or that the piece with a white thread on the side is the "blue fish".

Concentration: the child needs to pay attention to the card and the pieces, which helps to develop the ability to concentrate.

Social skills: using this toy with parents or other children helps develop social skills such as sharing, cooperating and learning to follow rules.

Taking this opportunity, since the subject is magnetism, I will tell you a story about Albert Einstein (1879-1955). According to his autobiographical notes, when he was 5 years old and recovering from an illness, his father gave him a compass and a magnet that fascinated him. Einstein did not understand how the compass needle changed position when he approached the magnet. Later, he would have said that that experience had profoundly marked his life!

Although there is no conclusive evidence, it is known that Einstein's father was a merchant who would have had access to scientific instruments. However, there are no records or documents that support the story of the compass. Even so, it is undeniable that Einstein was a scientific genius. In 1905, he published four works that revolutionized the world of physics, for this reason, 1905 is considered "the year of Einstein's miracle". One of these works, the "Theory of Relativity", opened the doors of knowledge, revealing the secrets of space, time and gravity. His discoveries had and continue to have a transformative impact on physics and other areas of knowledge. While the compass story may not be true, it remains a powerful illustration of how simple experiments can spark scientific curiosity.

In summary, toys that use magnetism can be fun and educational activities that help children develop physical, cognitive and social skills while having fun.

Albert Einstein: image available under the Creative Commons CC0 1.0 Universal Public Domain Dedication terms.

Material to make the "Fishing Game"

Materials that are part of the Kit "For Parents and Children"

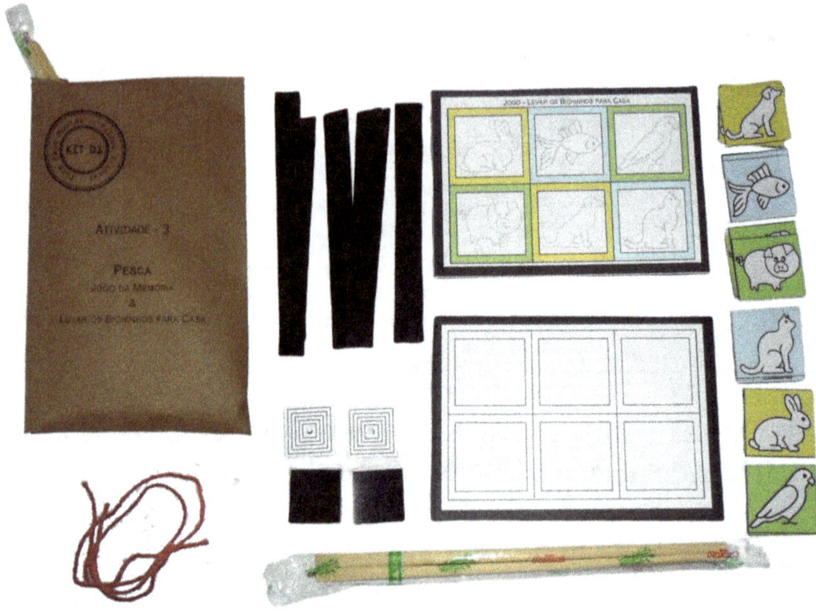

Inside the envelope you will find **8** magnetic strips measuring 1.3 x 12.5 cm; **4** cards for two different games; **18** magnetic rectangles measuring 3.5 x 3 cm with drawings of 6 animals, **2** square papers measuring 2.5 x 2.5 cm with a hole in the center; **2** square magnetic stickers 2.5 x 2.5 cm; **1** chopsticks and **2** strings.

If you purchase the Kit, do not give the envelope to your children. For this experience to present positive results, the parents must assemble the toy and the child must watch and help in the assembly.

To assemble a toy, you will need the following materials:

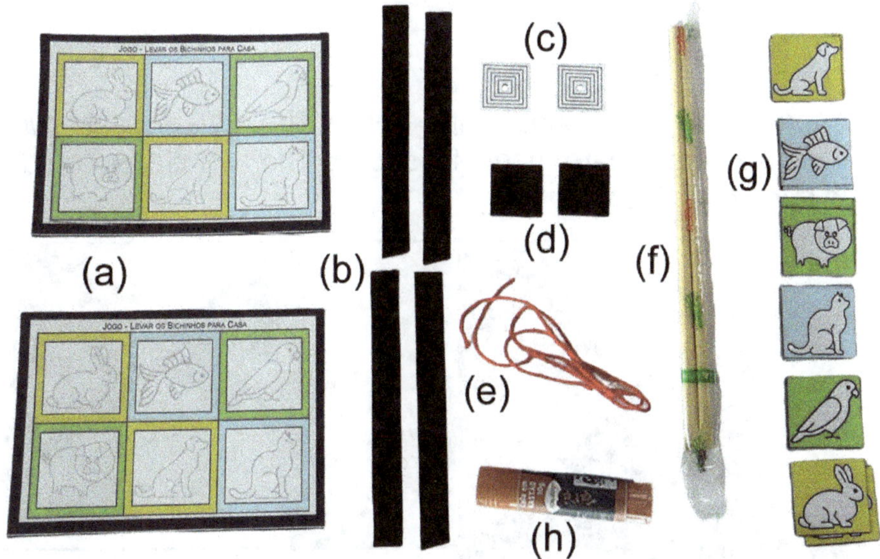

a) 2 cards from one of the games

b) 4 magnetic strips 1.3 x 12.5 cm

c) 2 square papers 2.5 x 2.5 cm with a hole in the center

d) 2 magnetic stickers 2.5 x 2.5 cm

e) 2 strings

f) 1 chopsticks

g) 18 magnetic rectangles with drawings of 6 animals.

h) glue stick

Fishing Game

Step by Step

One end of the string should fit between the square paper with the hole and the square magnetic sticker. The two pieces are the same size, 2.5 x 2.5 cm.

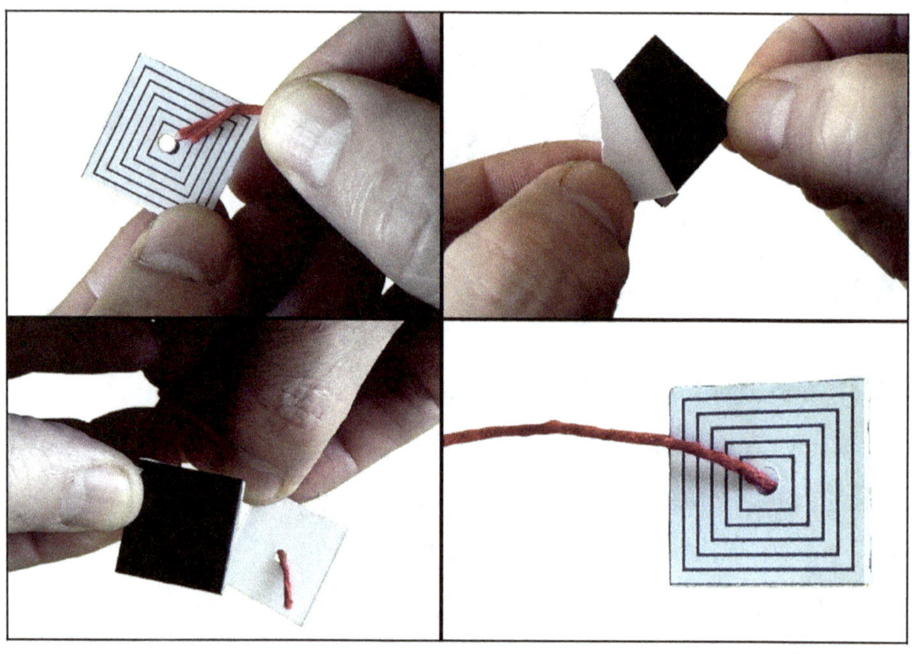

Thread the end of the string through the hole in the square paper, remove the magnetic adhesive backing, and glue the two parts together to secure the end of the string between the paper and the magnet. Do this procedure with 2 strings.

YouTube - step-by-step instructional video.

Split the chopsticks in half and tie the two strings at the thin ends. The game needs 2 "fishing rods".

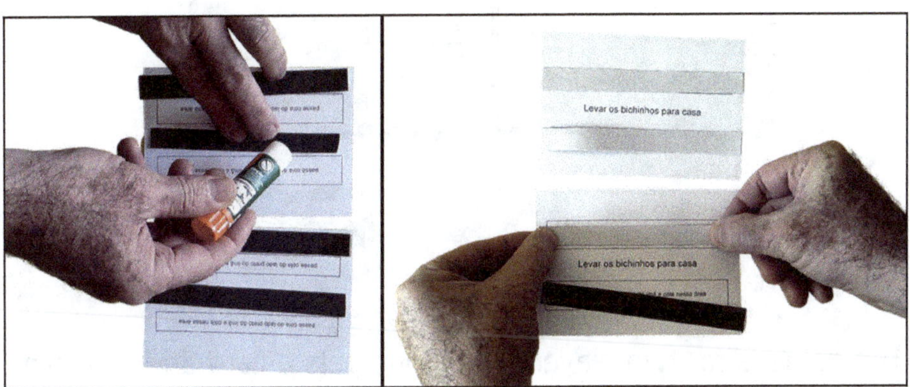

Apply glue **to the black side** of the magnetic strips and stick to the back of the cards. The Kit contains 8 magnetic strips and 4 cards. You need to stick two magnetic strips on the back of the cards.

Games with the "Fishing Game"

Game – "Take the Pets Home"

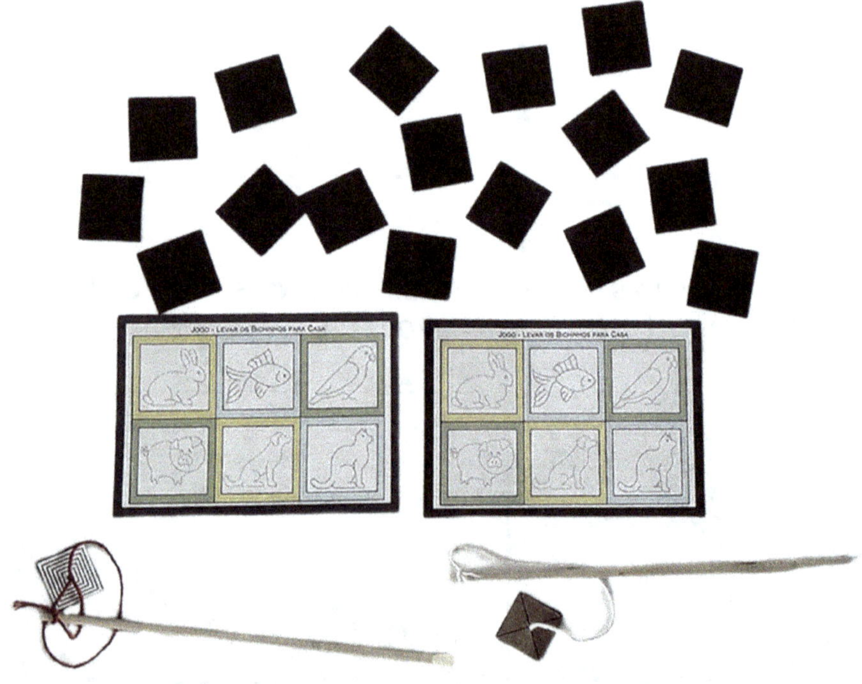

The game is for two players, each one gets a card and a "fishing rod". To play, the 18 magnetic rectangles must be spread out on a flat surface with the images facing down.

Each player, one at a time, uses their "fishing rod" to "fish" a pet. To do this, just touch the magnet on the "stick" to one of the 18 rectangles. It is important to remember that the images must be face down for the pieces to be attracted.

After "fishing", the player looks at the image and, if there is space on his card, he places the rectangle on it and passes the turn to the other player, and so on.

When a player "fishes" an animal that is already on his card, he leaves the rectangle next to the card and passes the turn to the other player.

The player who fills his card first wins the game.

For example

The player in the image on the left "caught" 3 repeated animals, while the player on the right "caught" only 1 repeated animal. As the player on the right filled his card, he won the game.

If all the rectangles happen to be "fished" and no player fills his card, the remaining rectangles go back to the table and the players continue to "fish" until one of them wins.

Memory game

Each player keeps 1 "fishing rod" and 1 card without drawings or colors.

Place the 18 magnetic rectangles on a flat surface with the designs facing down.

Each player, one at a time, will use their "fishing rod" to "fish" 4 rectangles. In the previous game, the player "fished" only 1 rectangle and passed the turn to the other player. In the memory game, each player needs to fish 4 rectangles in each move.

After "fishing", the player checks whether or not the drawings form a pair. If so, he places the same rectangles on his card.

The rectangles that do not form a pair are returned to the "table" of the game with the drawing facing down.

Whoever fills the card first wins the game.

Other games suggestions

Cooperative fishing

Parents and children play together using the 2 cards without the drawings. The objective is simply to "fish" the animals and place them on the cards.

Color game 1

You don't need to use the cards, the objective is to fish the rectangles and separate them by color.

Color game 2

Parents choose a color and the child tries to "fish" for animals of just the chosen color, it is a variation of the memory game. For example, the parents ask the child to "fish" only the animals with the yellow color, if it is not the chosen color, the child returns the "animal" to the pile and tries again. After catching 3 "little animals" of the same color, the parents choose a different color and the game starts again.

Fishing with stories

Tell a story while the child "fishes" the little animals. For example, if the child caught the "little pig", parents can tell the story of the

"3 Little Pigs", if they caught the dog – tell the story of Disney's "Lady and the Tramp", caught the cat – told the story of the "Aristocats" from Disney or make up a story, kids love stories and, in addition to being fun, parents will exercise their creativity and imagination.

Important

Not all the games indicated in this book will please the children. Remember to adapt suggestions to the child's skill level and always supervise the activities.

Activity 4

Equilibrist Butterfly

A balance-challenging toy is a great way to help a 4-year-old develop in different areas, including hand-eye coordination, curiosity, concentration, critical thinking, and problem solving skills. Here are some suggestions:

Motor coordination: the toy requires precise and coordinated movements to balance the butterfly on a base. This helps develop hand-eye coordination and the ability to use the body's muscles to execute precise movement.

Concentration: to use the toy successfully, the child needs to focus on the butterfly and the support base, which helps to develop their observation and concentration skills.

Critical thinking: when balancing the butterfly, the child will probably think "why" this happens, which helps to exercise observation and analysis skills.

Problem solving: most likely, the child will try to balance the butterfly in different places. This (natural) initiative helps to develop their ability to solve problems.

In addition, this is an activity that will help develop the child's imagination and creativity by encouraging them to explore and try different strategies for using the toy.

In short, the "Equilibrist Butterfly" is an educational toy that helps 4-year-olds develop motor, cognitive and problem-solving skills.

Material to make the Balancing Butterfly

Materials that are part of the Kit "For Parents and Children"

Inside the envelope you will find **2** butterflies; **4** rectangles with dotted lines, **2** toothpicks and **1** bottle cap with a hole in the center.

If you purchase the Kit, do not give the envelope to your children. For this experience to present positive results, the parents must assemble the toy and the child must watch and help in the assembly.

To assemble a toy, you will need the following materials:

a) 1 butterfly

b) 2 rectangles with dotted lines

c) 1 bottle cap with a hole in the center

d) 1 toothpick

e) glue stick

Equilibrist Butterfly

Step by Step

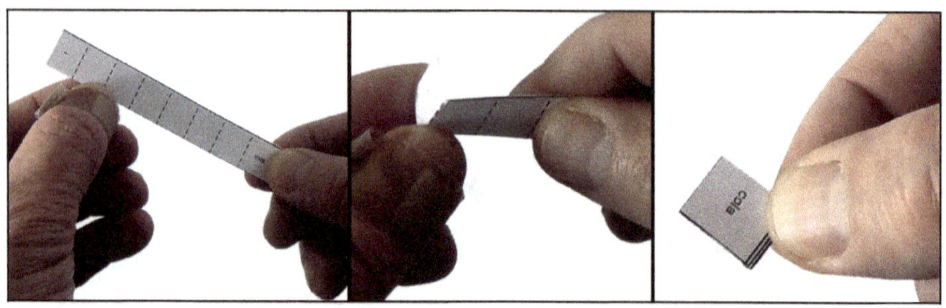

Fold two rectangles on the dotted lines, starting with the number 1 point.

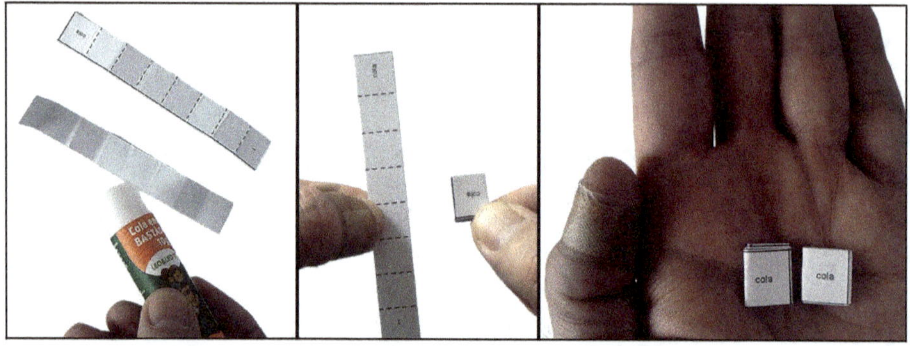

Open the paper, apply glue on the back and fold again. You will need to have two folded pieces of paper to use as a counterweight.

YouTube – Step-by-step instructional video.

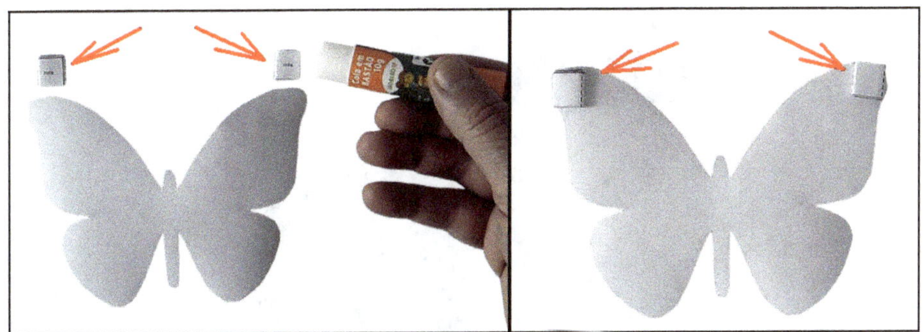

Glue the folded papers and stick them to the back of the butterfly, at the tips of the wings.

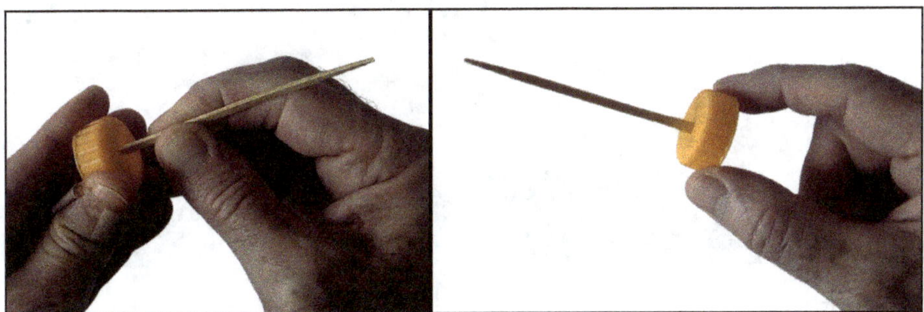

Fit the thicker end of the toothpick into the lid hole.

Caution: the toothpick is easy to break, hold the wood close to the end that will fit into the hole.

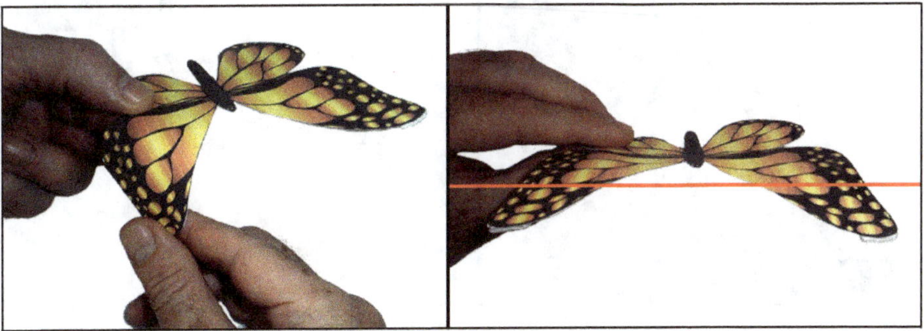

Fold the wing tips down a little. For the toy to work, the weights on the wings need to be positioned below the "butterfly head".

Teach the child to position the butterfly's head on the tip of the toothpick.

The best position is below the eyes, however, sometimes you need to put a little forward or backward to get the balance right.

Playing with the Equilibrist Butterfly

Balance game 1

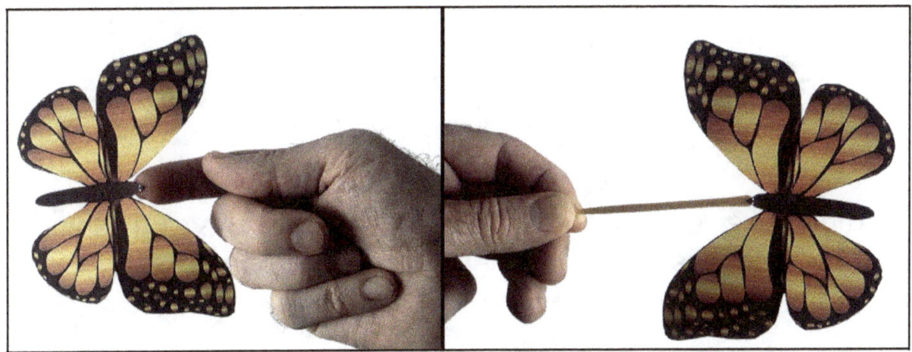

Have the child try to balance the butterfly in different places, such as on the tip of a finger, a pencil, or the toothpick they are holding.

Balance game 2

Once the butterfly is resting on the skewer, you can rotate it by pushing the wing tip very slowly. A fun game is to see who can make it spin the longest without falling off the stick.

Tip for rotating the butterfly

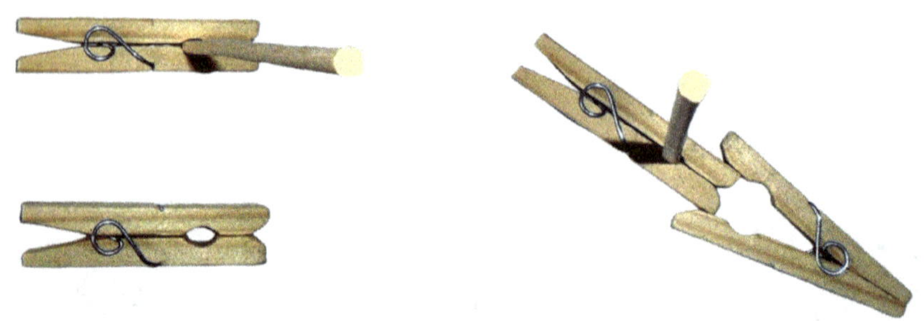

Fit the thicker end of one of the chopsticks to the clothespin. If the clothespin is not enough to hold the chopsticks, use two clothespins.

With great care, parents can cut a little bit off the sides of the butterfly's head to make the tip look like a triangle. Be careful not to cut the area where the eyes are located.

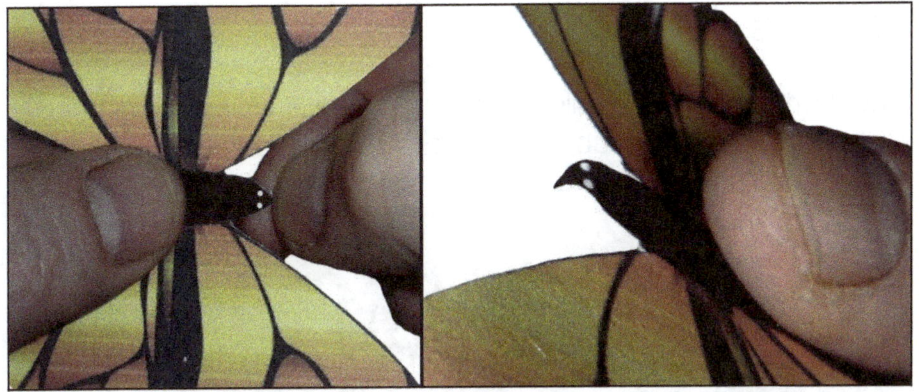

Use your fingernail to bend the tip of this "triangle" down. Make the fold exactly in the space between the tip of the triangle and the eyes of the butterfly.

Support the tip of the butterfly's head in the center of the stick and push the tip of the wing to make it rotate.

Balance path

The child, together with the parents, can walk to a certain point in the house and then return to the starting point with the butterfly on the tip of the finger or on a toothpick. The game is to make the round trip without letting the butterfly fall.

Balance dance

Play some music and ask the child to dance while balancing the butterfly on a fingertip or a stick. The game is to keep the butterfly balanced while dancing around the room.

You can screw the cap onto a PET bottle to make the butterfly taller.

How to make the toys in a simpler way

Tweezers

How to make the toy in a simpler way

The simplest form of this toy is to just use the clothespin to play the games suggested in the book. The child has fun and learns in the same way.

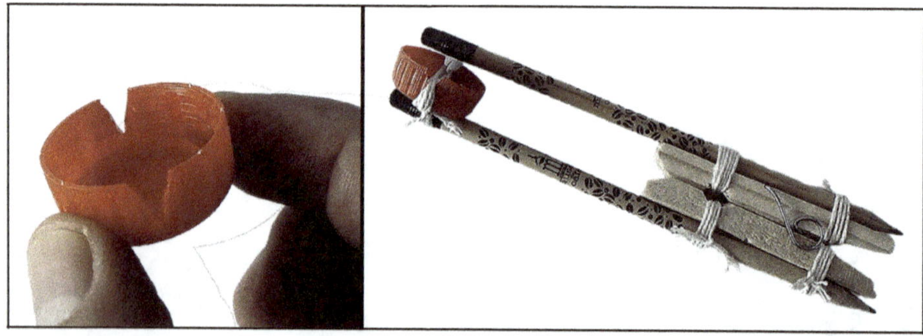

Instead of ice cream sticks, you can use 2 pencils or 2 pieces of cardboard cut into strips. The objects can be glued or tied around the clothespin. But, if you want to use the bottle cap, it needs to be glued, or you will have to make 2 cuts on the edge and tie with thread.

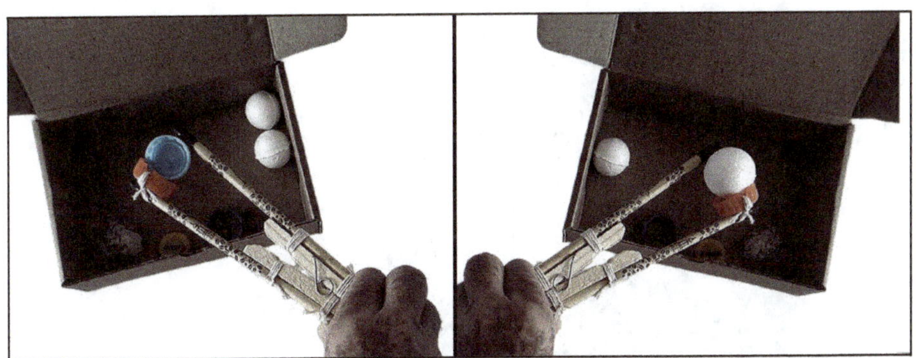

Also, it's important for children to watch their parents assemble the toys. Details such as adding a bottle cap, for example, can help stimulate children's imagination even more.

Polka Dot Launcher

How to make one with alternative materials

To assemble the toy, it is important to use a sturdy cardboard tube, such as those that come in PVC film, aluminum foil or parchment paper packaging. It is not recommended to use toilet paper tubes, as they are very thin and easily crumble under pressure from the rubber balloon or the player's hand.

The balloon is a fundamental material for the launcher to function. If you need to buy, choose a 9-inch size balloon, which is ideal for most tubes used.

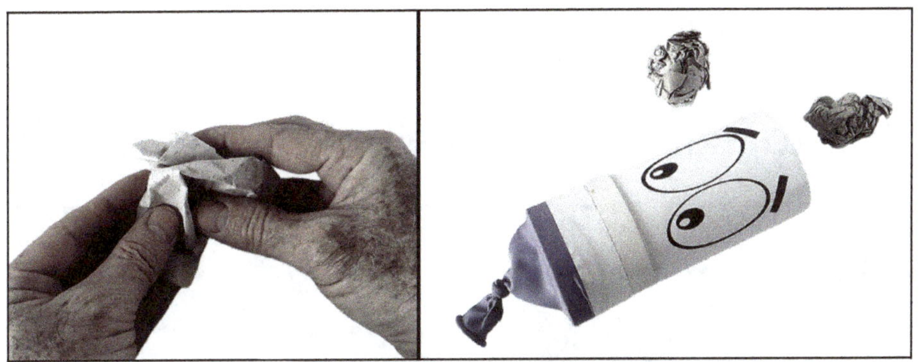

Balls can be made from crumpled paper.

After assembling the launcher, try the previously suggested pranks and have fun!

Fishing Game

How to make one with alternative materials

The magnet is an indispensable material for this activity. You can buy it in specialized stores or use "fridge magnets" that you already have at home. In some countries, companies advertise by distributing magnets to stick on fridges, you can use them to make the toy.

It is not necessary to have cards or drawings on the magnetic rectangles for the child to have fun. Just make a "fishing rod" by gluing a magnet to a piece of string tied to a pencil. Magnetism is a natural phenomenon that can be a great opportunity to stimulate children's imagination.

To make the game more sophisticated, you can draw a "card" on a piece of paper using geometric figures or colors and repeat the drawings on the magnets. Remember that the most important thing is to involve children in the assembling of the toys to develop curiosity and build confidence to put their creativity into practice.

Equilibrist Toy

How to make it with alternative materials

Activities that involve the center of mass or center of gravity (balance) are similar to the "Magnetic Fishing" toy. For children, toys that use the center of gravity seem like magic!

To do this activity, you will need a model. There are several free models available on the internet, for example, it is possible to make a tightrope walker by folding a sheet of paper, just follow the tutorial in the Qrcode.

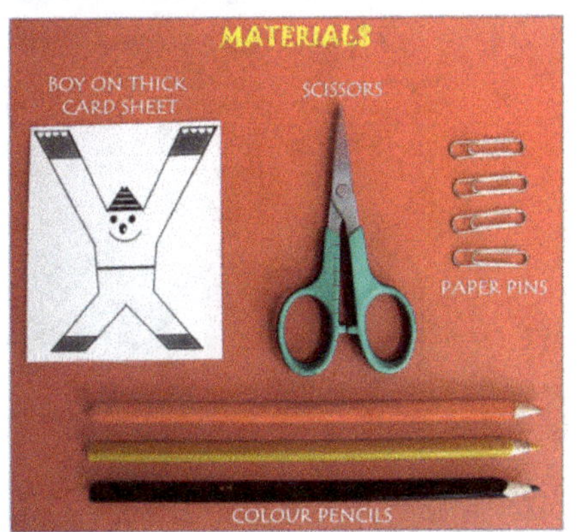

It is also possible to make a balancing clown following this other tutorial.

In addition to the balancing clown, the author of this idea also offers other activities that parents can do at home using simple and free materials. You can visit this proposal page by accessing the Qrcodes.

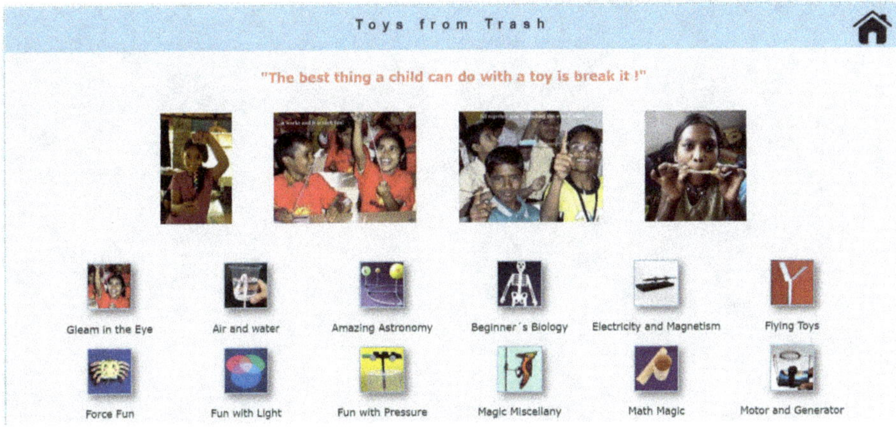

web site arvindguptatoys

Biography

I was born in 1960 in the city of São Paulo, Brazil, and I am passionate about history, science and philosophy. When I was 6 years old, with my mother's help, I built my first toy using materials that I had easy access to at home.

Among the various jobs I did during my life, I highlight the handouts in the IT area that I wrote in the 1980s; publications, games and digital applications in the 1990s, with emphasis on Almaque Abril on CD-ROM (Editora Abril) and the magazine CD-ROMania, launched in partnership with Editora Globo. At the beginning of the 21st century, after my son and niece's arrival, I dedicated myself to building toys and scientific experiments, which I made available free of charge - more than 1300 ideas with texts, images and explanatory videos - on the website "for parents and teachers".

In 2021, I had the opportunity to get to know up close the work that several NGOs develop in my country, when I graduated from Falcons University - NGO Gerando Falcões. Currently, I teach science and creativity to children aged 6 to 12 at Fundation Robson Montagna and I keep my facebook page active.

The book "Playing to create" is part of a larger project aimed at investing in global public education through an educational social network that will generate work and income in the less favored classes.

João Lino

facebook - Fundation Robson Montagna

facebook - for parents and teachers

web site - for parents and teachers